SPORTS CARS

- Colour Family Album -

This book is dedicated to Margaret Lenton with our thanks and appreciation.

Other Veloce publications -

Colour Family Album Series
Alfa Romeo by Andrea & David Sparrow
Bubblecars & Microcars by Andrea & David Sparrow
Bubblecars & Microcars, More by Andrea & David Sparrow
Citroën 2CV by Andrea & David Sparrow
Citroën DS by Andrea & David Sparrow
Fiat & Abarth 500 & 600 by Andrea & David Sparrow
Lambretta by Andrea & David Sparrow
Mini & Mini Cooper by Andrea & David Sparrow
Motor Scooters by Andrea & David Sparrow
Porsche by Andrea & David Sparrow
Vespa by Andrea & David Sparrow
VW Beetle by Andrea & David Sparrow
VW Beetle/Bug, Custom by Andrea & David Sparrow
VW Bus, Camper, Van & Pick-up by Andrea & David Sparrow

SpeedPro Series
How to Blueprint & Build a 4-Cylinder Engine Short Block for High Performance by Des Hammill
How to Build a V8 Engine Short Block for High Performance by Des Hammill
How to Build & Power Tune Weber DCOE & Dellorto DHLA Carburetors 2nd edition by Des Hammill
How to Build & Power Tune Harley-Davidson 1340 Evolution Engines by Des Hammill
How to Build & Power Tune Distributor-type Ignition Systems by Des Hammill
How to Build, Modify & Power Tune Cylinder Heads 2nd edition by Peter Burgess
How to Choose & Time Camshafts for Maximum Power by Des Hammill
How to Build and Modify Sportscar/Kitcar Suspension and Brakes by Des Hammill
How to give your MGB V8 Power Updated & Revised Edition by Roger Williams
How to Plan & Build a Fast Road Car by Daniel Stapleton
How to Power Tune BMC/BL/Rover 998cc A Series Engines by Des Hammill
How to Power Tune BMC/BL/Rover 1275cc A Series Engines by Des Hammill
How to Power Tune the MGB 4-Cylinder Engine by Peter Burgess
How to Power Tune the MG Midget & Austin-Healey Sprite by Daniel Stapleton
How to Power Tune Alfa Romeo Twin Cam Engines by Jim Kartalamakis
How to Power Tune Ford SOHC 'Pinto' & Sierra Cosworth DOHC Engines by Des Hammill

General
Automotive Mascots: A Collectors Guide to British Marque, Corporate & Accessory Mascots by David Kay & Lynda Springate
Bentley Continental Corniche & Azure 1951-1998 by Martin Bennett
Alfa Romeo Giulia Coupe GT & GTA by John Tipler
British Cars, The Complete Catalogue of 1895-1975 by Culshaw & Horrobin
British Trailer Caravans & their Manufacturers 1919-1959 by Andrew Jenkinson
British Trailer Caravans & their Manufacturers from 1960 by Andrew Jenkinson
Chrysler 300 - America's Most Powerful Car by Robert Ackerson
Cobra - The Real Thing! by Trevor Legate
Cortina- Ford's Best Seller by Graham Robson
Daimler SP250 'Dart' by Brian Long
Datsun/Nissan 280ZX & 300ZX by Brian Long
Datsun Z - From Fairlady to 280Z by Brian Long
Dune Buggy Hand Book, the by James Hale
Fiat & Abarth 124 Spider & Coupé by John Tipler
Fiat & Abarth 500 & 600 (revised edition) by Malcolm Bobbitt
Ford F100/F150 Pick-up by Robert Ackerson
Jim Redman - Six Times World Motorcycle Champion by Jim Redman
Grey Guide, The by Dave Thornton
Lea-Francis Story,The by Barrie Price
Lola - The Illustrated History (1957-1977) by John Starkey
Lola T70 - The Racing History & Individual Chassis Record New Edition by John Starkey
Mazda MX5/Miata 1.6 Enthusiast's Workshop Manual by Rod Grainger & Pete Shoemark
Mazda MX5/Miata 1.8 Enthusiast's Workshop Manual by Rod Grainger & Pete Shoemark
Mazda MX5 - Renaissance Sportscar by Brian Long
MGA by John Price Williams
Motor Museums - of the British Isles and Republic of Ireland by David Burke & Tom Price
Michael Schumacher - Ferrari Racing 1996-1998 by Braun/Schlegelmilch
Mini Cooper - The Real Thing! by John Tipler
Porsche 356 by Brian Long
Porsche 911R, RS & RSR New Edition by John Starkey
Porsche 914 & 914-6 by Brian Long
Prince & I, The (revised edition) by Princess Ceril Birabongse
Rolls-Royce Silver Shadow/Bentley T Series, Corniche & Camargue by Malcolm Bobbitt
Rolls-Royce Silver Wraith, Dawn & Cloud/Bentley MkVI, R & S Series by Martyn Nutland
Singer Story:Cars, Commercial Vehicles, Bicycles & Motorcycles by Kevin Atkinson
Taxi! The Story of the 'London' Taxicab by Malcolm Bobbitt
Triumph Tiger Cub Bible by Mike Estall
Triumph TR6 by William Kimberley
Volkswagen Karmann Ghia by Malcolm Bobbitt
VW Bus, Camper, Van, Pickup by Malcolm Bobbitt
Volkswagens of the World by Simon Glen
Works Rally Mechanic, Tales of the BMC/BL Works Rally Department 1955-1979 by Brian Moylan

First published 1999 by Veloce Publishing Plc., 33, Trinity Street, Dorchester DT1 1TT, England.
Fax: 01305 268864/e-mail: veloce@veloce.co.uk/website: http://www.veloce.co.uk
ISBN: 1-901295-27-3/UPC: 36847-00127-8

Readers with ideas for automotive books, or books on other transport or related hobby subjects, are invited to write to Veloce Publishing at the above address.
British Library Cataloguing in Publication Data -
A catalogue record for this book is available from the British Library.
Typesetting (Avant Garde), design and page make-up all by Veloce on AppleMac.
Printed in Hong Kong.

TRIUMPH

SPORTS CARS

- Colour Family Album -

VELOCE PUBLISHING PLC
PUBLISHERS OF FINE AUTOMOTIVE BOOKS

THANKS

Our grateful thanks to all the people who helped with this book -

Ken & Sue House, Don Pearce, Doug & Joan Sewell, Eric Hines, John Sullivan, John & Chris Vervecken-Selderslaghs, John Garlick, John Roberts, Steve & Carol Fitton, Alfred Widner, Dave & Marie Lewis, John & Mary Langford, Dave Chambers, Don & Audrey McCoy, John Canning, Paul Adkin, Oscar Yeo, Klaus Kistler, Ken & Diana Mulhall, Ralph Jones, Charlotte Weetman, Chris Balster, Primula de Havilland, Pat Lokatis, John Mumford, Lesley Phillips, Tara Scott, Trish Black, Claudia Die de Austin, Margarita Kazala, Patricia Monson, Marie Fyfe, Suzan Kaylan.

Coombe Abbey, The Arrow Mill & Restaurant near Alcester, Paul & Ann Corbett, Peter Lawrence at the *Slough Observer*, Frascati Restaurant at Chobham, Jacqui Fordham at the Heritage Motor Museum, Gaydon.

(TR7 1980)

CONTENTS

INTRODUCTION   6

1 TRIUMPH'S EARLY DAYS   7

2 TR2 & TR3   16

3 TR4, TR5 & TR6   29

4 TR7 & TR8   44

5 THE SPITFIRE   56

6 THE GT6   65

7 THE STAG   78

GALLERY   86

PHOTOGRAPHER'S
POSTSCRIPT   96

INTRODUCTION

Say 'name a Triumph sportscar,' and even someone with little interest in cars will probably be able to respond with 'Spitfire' or maybe even 'TR.' Triumph's sportscars have become very much a national icon over the years, as British as Sunday roast. However, the Triumph sportscar story is really very complex - the Spitfire's often neglected sibling, the GT6, has its own story to tell. Talking to a TR enthusiast will soon convince you that chalk and cheese are far too similar to describe the difference between the TR2 and the TR7. And yet despite the problems that were imposed upon them, the TR7 and 8, like the Stag, have a dedicated army of followers who would settle for nothing less.

(TR6 1972)

Getting all the Triumph enthusiasts we have met while preparing this book to agree on relative merits would be an impossible task, and a rather pointless one. However, there are several things that they do have in common - a tireless dedication to accurate restoration and sympathetic improvement, for example, and a willingness to help each other out - and not just those with an interest in the same model. They also tell some wonderful stories of Triumph ownership and driving experience, and with only a very slight emphasis on the discomfiture of MG owners.

As with other much-loved marques that are no longer in production, in any shape or form, there is a sense of preserving a complete piece of history. It is to the credit of Triumph enthusiasts everywhere that this preservation involves not just museum showpieces, but a whole lot of driving pleasure.

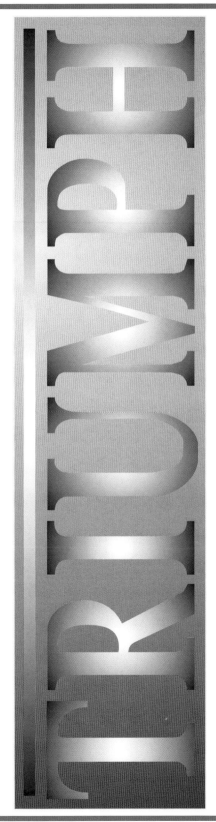

TRIUMPH'S EARLY DAYS

The Triumph company was formed in 1887 by Siegfried Bettmann, who had moved to Coventry from his native Germany four years previously. After two years in business selling bicycles, Bettmann actually started manufacturing his own product and decided that he needed a universal and easily remembered name for the company. Triumph produced its first motorcycle in 1902, with an associate company set up the following year in Germany to manufacture motorcycles there. Coincidentally, 1902 was also the year in which the Standard Motor Company - destined to take control of Triumph after the Second World War - was founded. Within a few years, Triumph motorcycle production was running at the rate of 20 a

The Gloria was the first really sporty Triumph, and set the scene for the TRs almost twenty years later. (Gloria Monte-Carlo 1934).

week, a figure which would rise to 60 by 1909. Triumph motorcycles began winning races too, with major successes in the TT events.

In 1913, Bettmann, who had immersed himself in the business and cultural life of Coventry, became the city's mayor for the year; a strange situation for him as war approached. Naturally the war interrupted every aspect of life, but Bettmann persuaded Colonel Claude Holbrook of the War Office that Triumphs should be the motorcycle of choice for the British Army. When the war was over Colonel Holbrook joined the Triumph company as General Manager (one of his particular aims was to get the company on track for producing a motor car).

The first Triumph car, the 10/21, went into production in 1923, and was available in both saloon and sports versions. The following year it was

Triumph would have liked to have taken on the world, and, had corporate fortune smiled on them a little more, they might have succeeded. (Gloria Monte-Carlo 1934).

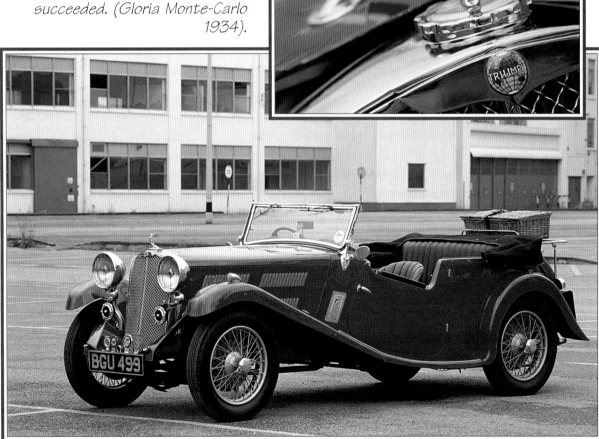

The Gloria Monte-Carlo was designed for rallying. It was narrower than the other Glorias, and carried two spare tyres at the rear. (Gloria Monte-Carlo 1934).

joined by a larger-engined version, the 13/35 (the first British-built car to be fitted with hydraulic brakes all round). In 1926 both were replaced by the more powerful 15/50 version, which two years on was renamed the Light 15, the last of which was built in 1930. By 1933, the Super Seven, which had been in production for 6 years, was given a higher specification and renamed the Super Eight. These cars were renowned racers, and their successes in rallying, with the likes of Donald Healey at the wheel, provided excellent publicity for the marque.

Triumph had also introduced the six cylinder Scorpion and the larger-bodied Twelve/Six, although neither were destined to become a Triumph success story by any measure. In their place, Triumph fitted the same chassis with a new four cylinder engine unit (with the body styles derived from their pred-

The Gloria was a great success and, although not inexpensive, was a car for the real motoring enthusiast. (Gloria Monte-Carlo 1934).

ecessors). These new cars, the Super Nine and the Super Ten, proved much better and more popular. In 1932, the Super Nine basics were fitted with a sporting body to give the Southern Cross - all three versions lasting until 1934. It was in this year, too, that Triumph produced a very small number of the Dolomite straight eight cars and the Gloria, which would remain in production for three years. The Gloria, a wonderful-looking car styled by Frank Warner, came in several different saloon and sporting versions, including the Gloria Vitesse, the Southern Cross Vitesse and the Monte-Carlo. The latter, which was designed particularly for rallying, sported a narrower bodywork and carried twin spare tyres at the rear.

Despite the undoubted successes, things were generally not going well for Triumph financially. In 1937 the company was relaunched with a new model range, which included a 1.5 litre Gloria, a Gloria-derived Vitesse, the Continental, and an exotically-styled Dolomite sporting the famous 'Waterfall' grille (this caused a great stir - loved and hated in equal measure). Two years later, Triumph attempted a move to the mass production car market, with a new Twelve, but the timing was sadly against them as the war intervened before the car had a chance to get off the mark. The company had, in any case, been over-ambitious in their assessment of the market for their cars generally, and was put into the hands of the receivers.

The Vale Special was built by a small firm in Maida Vale, London, using a Triumph chassis and an 832cc engine. More than 50 were made - this is number five, registered on Christmas Eve 1932. It is now powered by a Coventry Climax unit. (Vale Special 1932).

So controversial was the waterfall grille that Triumph offered a more conventional alternative for customers who couldn't live with it. (Dolomite 1938).

The Dolomite name first appeared on a Triumph in 1935, on the 'waterfall grille' cars. It would re-appear in 1970 on a rather less exotic Triumph. (Dolomite 1938).

Depending on your point of view, the Dolomite 'Waterfall' radiator grille is either breath-takingly beautiful or hideously ugly. It is certainly a very unusual feature on a non-American car. (Dolomite 1938).

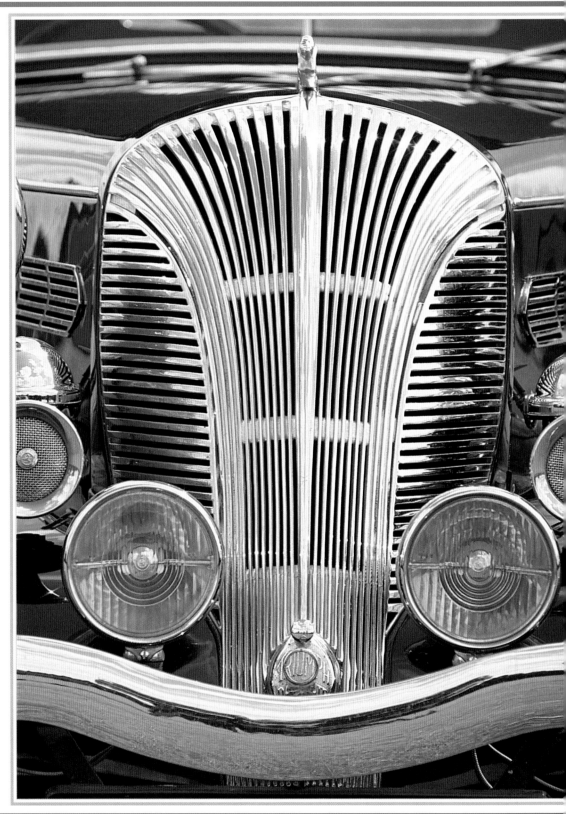

Once the war was over, Europe's car manufacturers needed to get back into production as quickly as possible. Triumph was purchased by the Standard Motor Company, and Managing Director Sir John Black was anxious to get his marques up and running without delay. Sir John had a long-standing dream of producing a car to take on the best - Jaguar and MG in particular - and he was a determined and forceful man who usually got his way. In 1946 Triumph launched the 1800 Town & Country Saloon, plus a Roadster version on a shortened wheelbase. The engine was initially the Standard 1800 unit, but this was soon replaced with the more powerful Vanguard 2000 engine. The Roadster had a strange little rumble seat which necessitated climbing over the rear wing in order to sit down. Although tall people might be ideally suited for the climb, the legroom available once they got there was rather limited. Although the saloon version soldiered on as the Renown - and spawned long wheelbase limousine versions to boot - the attractive Roadster did not survive into the fifties.

With smaller cars making an impact in the new decade, Triumph hoped that its offering, the Mayflower, would appeal on both sides of the Atlantic. However, although the car had genuine appeal, there was something decidedly pre-war about its image. It might appeal to the traditionalist, but it was never going to open up new horizons for Triumph (nor was it likely to make much headway in the USA either, since it cost more to buy than a home-grown Chevrolet). A cabriolet Mayflower bloomed briefly during 1950, but faded with only ten cars made (and the saloon was destined to last

Triumph's rather overambitious plan was for the roadster to take on the up-market Jaguars. (2000 Roadster 1949).

only until 1953).

Sir John Black's dream of building a top sportscar had so far come to nought, despite attempts with the lozenge-shaped TRX, of which only three were ever built.

At the Earls Court Motor Show in October 1952, however, Triumph unveiled the TR1, which was given a complete redesign from the ground up before it was launched onto the market the following year as the TR2. The legendary Triumph TR was on the road ...

The last production car to have a rumble seat - now a great hit with little bridesmaids when the car is used for weddings! (2000 Roadster 1949).

The Roadster was a beautiful car with elegant lines. This example has been restored to its original condition by Doug Sewell. (2000 Roadster 1949).

TR2 & TR3

The TR2, styled by Walter Bedgrove, was a charming car with character. It was fun to drive, without being too thirsty, and unlike previous Triumph offerings, it was priced right for the market. Its competitive price was due, in part, to the use of readily available components from other cars from the same stable - a method of building sometimes unkindly labelled 'parts bin special' - but then, why re-invent the wheel? The TR's two litre (1991cc) four cylinder wet liner engine unit came courtesy of the Standard Vanguard - which had in turn inherited it from the Ferguson tractor, although needless to say tuning was undertaken at each stage! In TR guise, the engine produced a respectable 90bhp - enough to give the little car plenty of 'go.' A

Classic British sportscar of the 50s - the TR2 looks good, and driving it will put a smile on your face. (TR2 1955).

four speed version of the three speed Vanguard gearbox was fitted, the chassis was a lengthened and reinforced version of that of the Standard Nine, and the rear axle and front suspension came from the Mayflower. The TR's body panels, and therefore its character, were entirely new.

The first TR2, introduced in 1953, was not without its problems though. Owner Eric Hines recalls that it was impossible to take a girl out on a date in one - particularly to Leamington Spa! The kerbs

The TR's interior was plain, uncluttered and stylish. (TR2 1955).

When Eric Hines bought his TR2 in 1991, it had been partially restored. Eric finished the job, and the car is now better than new. (TR2 1955).

There had never been a car quite like the TR before - Triumph had found a winning formula. (TR2 1955).

The TR2's engine was the 1991cc from the Standard Vanguard, based on a unit first used in the Ferguson tractor. (TR2 1955).

were just too high for the doors, and if the bottoms of the doors were to remain unscathed, street credibility would be lost as the proud owner tried to find a practical stopping place without kerbs. Fortunately, Triumph came to the rescue, in late 1954, with a short door modification; a perfect cure for most towns - Leamington Spa now only needing a modicum of caution! There were improvements to the rear brakes too, and the option of overdrive was introduced - a well received addition to the refinement process in the opinion of many owners. Cosmetically, one could specify a leather interior, wire wheels, rear wing spats, and stiffer, sports-style suspension. Most important of all, for an English sportscar, was the option of a detachable hardtop (although it was relatively inexpensive, Triumph could not afford to let the TR become just a fair weather second car - it needed all round appeal if it was to be a marketing success). The TR2 did indeed sell well; by October 1955, when the TR3 superceded it, more than 8600 had been sold in all.

The most obvious difference in looks between the TR2 and the TR3 was the addition of a grille cover - a small change in metal terms, but one which made a great difference to the character of the car. The engine was also upgraded to give 95bhp, and then almost immediately the process was repeated to give 100bhp. The TR3 was a sprightly little car as a result, the effect heightened by the fitting of disc brakes on the front - the first British production car to be so equipped, and another milestone for the TR. In all, the TR3 was a much nicer car for day to day driv-

The first production TR - the full depth door would hit pavement kerbs, and was soon replaced with a shorter door version. (TR2 1953).

The most obvious difference between the TR2 and TR3 was the addition of a radiator grille. (TR3 1956).

The TR3 had a friendly face, but not everyone preferred its looks to the TR2. (TR3 1956).

ing than the TR2 had been, although many people preferred - and still do prefer - the looks of the TR2. 13,300 customers bought the TR3, however, and a huge number - 60,000 - purchased the car that replaced it, or perhaps one should say evolved from it.

The TR3A was far and away the most popular of the early TRs. All those niggling little problems that beset a newly introduced car - and some that were potentially a lot more serious - had been solved. The TR3A really was a lovely little car, and often the only thing missing, in Britain anyway, was good weather for driving around in open top fashion. As for looks, the TR3A was the first in the series with a wide-mouthed grille. This new feature, along with the 'eye' headlamps - set further back than on previous TRs, gave the TR3A an unmistakable face; its fans instantly recognised the friendly character with the cheeky grin. Exterior doorhandles, previously a GT pack option, became standard, as did a boot catch.

However, despite the car's obvious appeal, sales began to drop off by the beginning of the sixties. The trend was for better fixtures and more comfort, and Triumphs' competition was beginning to offer just that. The TR had to change if it was to survive. When the change came, however, there was a brief swansong for the TR3. When the new TR4 came along,

The TR3 was the first British production car to be fitted with front disc brakes - when you have 100bhp under your hood, it's good to know you can stop too. (TR3 1956).

British weather dictates a well fitting hood for any open top car - and it should be as quick and easy to put up as possible. (TR3 1956).

Although British to the core, TRs were built elsewhere too - this left hand drive TR3 at Nonceveaux in Belgium. (TR3 1956).

This TR3's indigo blue paintwork is a Jaguar colour rather than a Triumph one - but it suits the car down to the ground. (TR3 1956).

Because of its simplicity, the dash of the early TR looks classic rather than dated. (TR3 1956).

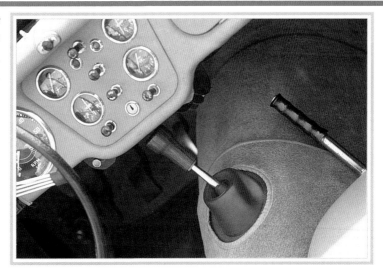

The TR3A was a very popular buy; the teething problems with the earlier cars had all been sorted out, and most owners found driving the car sheer pleasure. (TR3A 1959).

Originally powder blue, this TR3A has been restored in British Standard Royal Blue - an original colour option when the car was built. (TR3A 1959).

US dealers - more conservative about things British than the British themselves - weren't sure it would sell well. Triumph, therefore, gave the TR3 a final push, with a model that would become known as the TR3B. This ruse also had the advantage of using up the very last of the earlier body shells - all 3300 of them to be precise. The first 500 or so TR3Bs were virtually identical to the TR3A, but the remainder - fitted with the new TR4 engine and gearbox - have become one of the most sought after of all the TRs. This was partly due to the fact that so few were made, but it was also because they represented the last, and thus the most fully developed, of the first generation of TRs.

In the fifties there was (and there still is), a good deal of rivalry between TR and MG enthusiasts. A popular T-shirt of the period proclaimed: 'I'd rather be pushing a Triumph than driving an MG.' In the early days, it was the done thing for MG drivers to remark with a jeer that the competition handled appallingly - to which the Triumph riposte was, 'put a decent engine in your car, and it would handle worse!' Whatever the truth behind these exchanges, it was undeniable that the little Triumph was a very characterful, very British little sportscar. If it was going to survive and prosper through the 1960s, though, it was going to have to evolve.

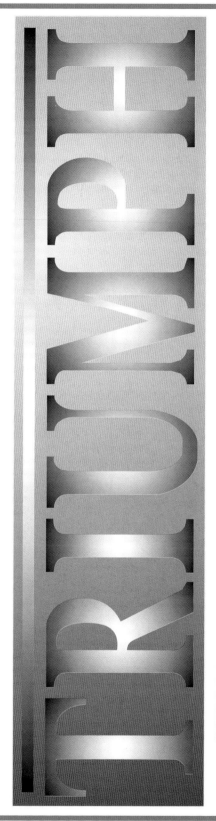

TR4, TR5 & TR6

Cars were changing fast in the mid 1950s, both mechanically and style-wise, and the market for small sportscars was not so great that Triumph could afford to be left behind. Sir John Black had been replaced as head of the company by Alick Dick, and the old guard gave way to a more progressive and forward-looking team. In 1956, they were introduced to the up-and-coming Turin-based designer Giovanni Michelotti, who had all the qualities they were looking for: he was innovative, receptive and practical, and he could work fast. Michelotti set to work on several projects for Triumph, including the preliminary work on a new image for the TR. He produced several one-off styling exercises over the next few years, including the Zest

The Michelotti-designed TR4 had great styling similarities to the TR3. The full-width grille, though, gave the new car a very different face. (TR4A 1967).

and Zoom prototypes, but, although Triumph management liked what they saw, they never quite went as far as sanctioning the next stage of the process. By 1960, however, they realised they had to commit. Michelotti was given a final brief, based on elements of the one-off cars, and soon had two prototypes ready for testing. The first new TR4s rolled off the production line in September 1961, with full-scale production getting up to speed by the start of the following year.

Although a new chapter of TR story began with the TR4, the car was by no means an all new production.

The TR4 chassis was a modified version of that of its predecessor, with extra side members to accommodate the rack and pinion steering. The suspension comprised coil springs and wishbones at the front, and semi-elliptic springs at the rear. The engine was the same unit that had powered the previous TRs, but enlarged in capacity to 2138cc, giving increased power of 100bhp, although the smaller 1991cc unit remained an option for those who preferred it. One item, however, that was all new for the TR4, was the fully synchro-mesh four speed gearbox.

The styling was all new too, although the friendly and popular shape of the original TR had not been abandoned completely. The new shape provided more room for driver and passengers, more boot space, and more mechanic-friendly access to the working parts. The interior fittings were improved, as was the placing of the instruments. A softtop was standard TR4 issue, but an optional hardtop was available for winter use. A third option was the Michelotti-designed Surrey top - a pre Targa affair with a fixed rear window section and remov-

The new engine was a 2138cc unit, although the old 1991cc was still available for those who preferred it. (TR4A 1967).

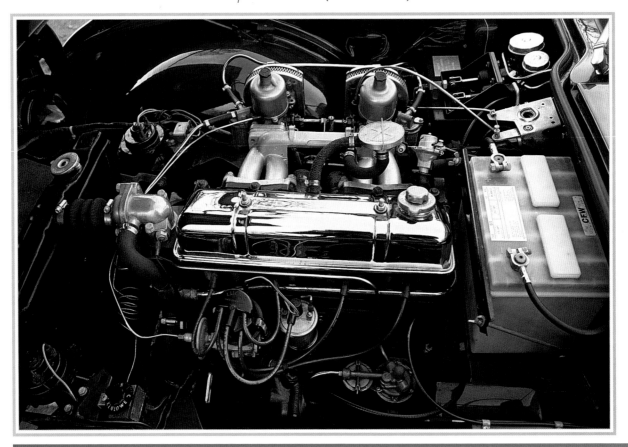

The TR4A was updated with an improved dashboard and completely redesigned centre console. (TR4A 1967).

The US market was unhappy with the introduction of independent rear suspension, so a hybrid was provided to keep them happy. Cars with the new suspension were identified by the 'IRS' script on the boot. (TR4A 1967).

The TR5
version for
the home
and
European
market was
the PI
(Petrol
Injection).
At 150bhp,
it could
really fly.
(TR5 PI
1968).

able panel. The problem with this latter option was that the panel was too large for the luggage compartment. This restricted the usefulness of an otherwise perfect compromise - a decision on the weather had to be made before starting out!

Although the TR4 was very popular - in three and a half years, more than 40,000 were sold - it also came in for a good deal of criticism (in terms of the harshness of its ride, and its less-than-perfect steering characteristics). The men at the top - a different set of faces, now headed by Stanley Markland and Donald Stokes - decided that a new chassis was in order, and so the TR4A hit the drawing board.

The first TR4A models appeared at the beginning of 1965. The key to the new design was its independent rear suspension, courtesy of the Triumph 2000. Apart from this, the only other changes were cosmetic: new badges and a slightly altered grille; updated lamp housings; improved dashboard and redesigned centre console.

The TR4A had a production run of over 28,000, with few changes to the design along the way. However, American dealers were unimpressed with the independent rear suspension from the start, and were provided with a TR4/TR4A hybrid to keep them happy, although the IRS version was available in the USA as an option for those that wanted it.

It had been obvious, almost from the car's introduction, that the TR4A was not a

The Surrey top from Michelotti - a fixed rear window with removable mid panel, similar in design to the Porsche Targa... (TR5 PI 1968).

...a good idea, which would have been perfect if the removable section fitted in the boot. (TR5 PI 1968).

The Michelotti TRs are instantly recognisable from their full-width 'smile.' (TR5).

long-term solution. The engine was showing its age, customers were starting to demand something more upmarket, and American legislation covering specifications could not be ignored. During the early sixties, a few TR4 prototypes had been fitted with the six cylinder engines which powered the Vitesse, and later the GT6. The experiment was now developed further, with a view to appointing the successor to the TR4A. In truth, Triumph knew that they had to do something rather more radical with the TR series than add a couple of cylinders to the engine. However, they also knew that this would not be an overnight job.

In the meantime, it became apparent that the American situation needed to be addressed before customers were lost. The TR5 would need to come in two versions - one with a US-legal specification, and another for the home market and elsewhere. Introduced in 1967, the US version, called the TR250, came with a 2498cc engine fitted with dual carburettors and produced just 104bhp. Despite some modernising touches - a black dash and bonnet stripes, for example, as well as the change of engine - the TR250 offered very little that had not been available

Fitted with dual carburettors to meet legal standards, the engine of the US version of the TR5, the TR250, could produce only 104bhp, against 150bhp from the UK version. (TR250 1968).

on the TR4A. Also, the relative lack of power did little to help sales.

The home market and the rest of the world got the TR5PI - same engine, but with fuel injection resulting in a power boost to 150bhp. The model had begun to show its age, however, and sales of the TR5PI struggled to reach 3000, although the TR250 made it to 8500 in the eighteen months that it was produced.

Work on the longer-term TR evolution began even before the TR5/250 was introduced. Even with this new TR6, the design team were not working with a completely clean sheet. The basics of the car were to remain as before, but there was to be a major facelift. Michelotti was too busy to take on the work, but the Karmann company were able to do it, and had the added advantage of having

the facilities for prototype building, testing and even bodyshell manufacture. Karmann had also built up a reputation for fast work, and their approach to the TR6 task was no exception. They had the major part of the work completed within a year, and the first TR6 rolled off the production line in the last quarter of 1968.

Karmann's work on the TR involved leaving the centre

The underpowered TR250 was more popular than the home-market version - it could have done even better with more real zip in place of the go-faster stripes.
(TR250 1968).

This tasty Damson Red TR6 was built in Mechelen, Belgium. (TR6 1972).

The Karmann treatment left the centre section of the car largely unchanged from the TR5, but radically redesigned both front and rear. (TR6 1972).

Midway through the TR6's production life, a new rear flank badge proudly proclaimed its country of origin. (TR6 from 1973).

Opposite - The TR6 first put in an appearance in 1968, and remained in production for eight years. (TR6 1972).

section largely untouched, but refashioning the bodywork front and rear. This resulted in a more modern, more angular, shape. Most of the mechanicals, though, were unchanged from the TR5, although wider wheels and an anti-roll bar improved the handling. There was a detuned version for America, although both versions were known as TR6 (the home market fuel injected cars being officially designated TR6PI). The public took to the new TR in a big way. More than 90,000 were built during a production run of almost eight years, the vast majority in US spec form. There were few changes to the car during this time - seats and wheels were improved in 1970, and 1973 brought a front spoiler and Union Jack rear flank badge.

The biggest changes of all happened not to the car, but to the company. Triumph had been under British Leyland's umbrella since the early sixties, all the holdings of which were absorbed into one large conglomerate in 1968. By the mid-seventies, however, British Leyland was in dire financial straights (only rescued by nationalisation). It is with this major change in Triumph's structure and fortunes that this chapter of the TR story draws to a close.

Opposite - The TR6 was hugely popular, especially in the USA. Had the company been weathering the storms better, it could have been the start of something even bigger. (TR6 1973).

Above: From 1973, the TR6 gained a small spoiler under the front bumper. (TR6 1973).

TR7 & TR8

There are those who would contend that the TR story really ended with production of the final TR6, and that the two final cars to carry the TR name are neither worthy successors, nor part of the real TR family. However, it was under this badge that British Leyland chose to market them. While they may not have the old fashioned British sportscar feel that endeared TRs 2 through 6 to thousands of enthusiasts, it is worth considering that these cars were not perfect, and the 7s and 8s were not without their good points, nor without an enthusiastic following of their own.

Everything about the new TR7 differed from that of its predecessor. Had it been called something else entirely, it would probably not have had to contend with so many

The TR7 arrived in 1975 - a year before the TR6 was withdrawn, and remained in production until the end of the TR series in 1981. (TR7 1980).

negative comparisons. It was, after all, initially only available in coupe form; the Leyland 2000 coupe might have met with a better reception. A common complaint about the early TRs was that changes were introduced very slowly and cautiously, even when they appeared to be long overdue. Conversely, the TR7 was criticised for its quantum leap - it appeared to have nothing of the past about it. The TR7 was of monocoque construction, with a solid rear axle. It was fitted with a 1998cc four cylinder engine. The major difference between home market and US versions was in the type of carburettor used, the home market cars having power figures of 105bhp against the US version's 90bhp. The TR7 was a comfortable car, with excellent seats, and a roomy and well-appointed interior. Although it lacked a degree of power, it handled well and could be fun to drive. On the downside, however, the cars were plagued with problems, most of them due not to any inherent problem with the design, but rather to the appalling lapses in build quality and quality control that plagued Leyland at that time. Cars built at the Liverpool plant were particularly infamous in this respect, their outline 'TR7' bonnet decal signifying to potential second-hand buyers to take extra care.

The first TR7s rolled off the production line in 1975, overlapping with the TR6 by almost a year. A convertible was introduced in 1979 - rather too late perhaps, since this was the version of the TR7 that had the most instant appeal, and could have been held out as a radical, but realistic, alternative open-topped sportscar to

Build problems made the TR7 a doubtful second-hand buy. It is only quite recently that the TR7 and TR8 have come into their own as classics. (TR7 1980).

the previous TRs. There were two special edition convertible TR7s, the Spider and the Victory, their specialities being cosmetic - special paint and trim.

Leyland conceived the TR8 as a sportscar to win back the TR credibility. It might have done just that too, if the company had been in better overall shape, and able to support it with expertise and customer confidence. The Rover 3528cc V8 engine was certainly up to the task: 148bhp giving a top speed of 120mph, and a zero to 60mph time of 8.4 seconds (these figures are for US cars - home market cars had slightly more power). It may not have been the zenith of performance, but certainly needed no apology. In 1978 and 1979 only coupes were made, and in small numbers, but by 1980 the convertible was introduced. The TR8 lasted only until 1981, when the TR7 was also withdrawn. Only 3000 or so TR8s were made, the vast majority of these going to the US. The TR7 and the TR8 both suffered from the reputation that the first TR7s had earned, and from the equally bad reputation of Leyland as a company. At a different time, and with different backup, they could have been the precursors of more models carrying the TR badge.

As things turned out, however, they brought the TR story to a rather downbeat conclusion.

Paul Adkin is a TR8 enthusiast. The car he now owns was originally exported to Phoenix Arizona, where it was bought by a United States Airforce flight mechanic, and used in the US until 1983. The owner was then stationed to Upper Heyford in Gloucestershire and took the car to England with him. He decided to sell the car, and put a note in the window to that effect. He left the car parked in Leamington Spa one day, where the 'For Sale' sign was spotted by would-be TR8 owner Paul. Frustratingly, the telephone number had no area code with it, but Paul noticed that a US pilot's magazine had been left on the dashboard. Paul put two and two together and finally located the owner at the Upper Heyford airbase. He was soon the proud owner of a TR8! Paul, who was an impoverished student at the time, used the car as daily transport for a year before he could afford to start his restoration project. With many other demands on his time, Paul spent ten long years restoring his TR8 - but the results are certainly worth the wait - a testimony to the virtues of perseverance and patience!

Leyland had great hopes for their TR7/8 series, but failed to address build quality problems. (TR7 1980).

Whereas UK buyers got 105bhp from the TR7's 1998cc engine, US owners were only allowed 90bhp. (TR7 1981).

Opposite - The TR7 was actually a very good looking car. Perhaps it should not have been given the TR name, with all the expectations that it brought. (TR7 1981).

Had the topless TR7 been introduced at the start, the car might have got a better reception. (TR7 1981).

This car started life as a left hand drive TR7. It had two owners before being restored and updated to re-emerge as a right hand drive TR8 with US spec, including airconditioning, and a V8 engine - and it has done less than 12,000 miles from new!

The car which Paul Adkin strove so hard to own... (TR8 1979)

...both car and driver are in their element on the open road. (TR8 1979).

Only coupes were built in 1978/79, although a small number of convertibles were built in 1980. (TR8 1979).

Only 3000 TR8s were built - most went to the States - Paul Adkin's has come home to the UK. (TR8 1979).

With its Rover V8 3528cc engine, the TR8 had great potential - with an 8.4 second 0 to 60 time and a top speed of 120mph, it was no sluggard. (TR8 1979).

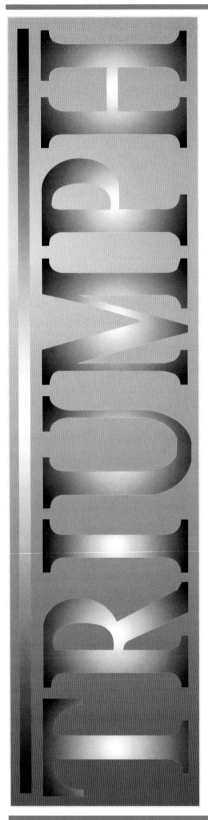

THE SPITFIRE

The Michelotti-designed Triumph Herald was introduced in 1959, initially as a two plus two coupe with a four cylinder 948cc engine. This was soon joined by the saloon, a true four seater, and by the convertible in 1960. The Herald was a charming little car that offered a full four seats (though back seat passengers couldn't be too large), and a hood that almost completely disappeared when folded down. For 1961, a bigger engine option - the 1200cc - arrived, which gave the car a welcome boost of power. Estate and van options would also be offered, as well as the 12/50, a saloon with a 50bhp version of the 1200cc engine, the beefed up chassis from the Vitesse, a folding

The Spitfire was based on the Triumph Herald. One of the remarkable features of both convertibles was that the hood disappeared from view when lowered. (Herald convertible 1965).

sunroof and distinguishing trim. Soon all the other Heralds were using this chassis, and were fitted with a 48bhp version of the engine. The Herald got a 1300cc engine in 1968, and a front styling overhaul courtesy of Vitesse panels - an easy enough procedure as the car's bodywork was comprised of bolt-on sections. The 1200 continued alongside this 13/60 Herald for a while, but soon suffered at its hands, and was withdrawn in 1970. The final Heralds lasted for another year before production ended.

As soon as the Herald was introduced, Triumph began to look at the idea of an inexpensive sportscar based on it. Michelotti worked on the idea and came up with an appealing design, but it was felt that the time was not right to push the project forward, and the experimental prototype gathered dust in the corner. However, with the advent of Leyland's involvement, it was hauled out, reappraised, and was soon approved for production. The first Spitfire, later to become known as the Mk I, was introduced in 1962. It was fitted with a 63bhp incarnation of the 1200 Herald engine (actually 1147cc). The Herald chassis was adapted for the Spitfire, and given a rigid backbone by moving the side members to the centre. A problem of this arrangement, however, was that the car relied for its rigidity on the strength of the welded sills. Consequently, ignored and rusted sills would have a terminal effect on the car, and made any kind of good major repair a very expensive option.

The Spitfire was well received. It offered good sportscar motoring at an affordable price. The car's handling might not have been 100%, but then the Spitfire was not meant to be a leading

The first Spitfire arrived in 1962. The Mk II, which came three years later, had a little more power, plus refinements to the interior. (Spitfire Mk II 1965).

Initially well-received, the Spitfire's popularity has increased through the years. (Spitfire Mk II 1965).

Open-top motoring is wonderful, but one must be practical. A hardtop was introduced with the Mk II - a must for a British sportscar! (Spitfire Mk II 1965).

Opposite - When the sun stopped shining, the Mk III Spitfire was easily covered up, thanks to an excellent new folding hood frame. (Spitfire Mk III 1967).

Ken and Diana Mulhall's labour of love - from fungus infested rust-bucket to pristine Spitfire - in three years of very hard work. (Spitfire Mk III 1967).

edge sportscar - it was meant to be fun. And it was fun, with excellent front suspension for a good sporty ride, as well as small touches that the competition lacked - proper windows for example, and the space to carry real luggage. There would be few major changes during the Spitfire's eighteen year lifespan - its development was more a programme of continuing improvement and refinement (including measures needed to meet US emission laws). The Mk II was introduced in 1965. Engine power was increased to 67bhp, the interior was more comfortable, and a well-designed removable hardtop extended the Spitfire driving season into the winter months.

The Triumph Spitfire Mk III was introduced to the public in January 1967. The engine boasted another boost in power, to 75bhp, thanks to an increase in engine capacity to 1296cc. There were several other changes made at the same time: an improved level of interior trim, folding hood frame, and new-style higher bumpers, which changed the face of the Spitfire consider-ably. As a stopgap measure, the first batch of Mk III Spitfires was fitted with a full-width radiator courtesy of the Herald 1200, and the hood was fastened in place using Herald/Vitesse style catches. 1971 brought the Spitfire in Mk IV form, the major difference from the Mk III being the chopped rear end styling and full width bumper, which brought the Spitfire more into line, shape-wise, with its stablemates. There was also a new rear suspension setup which brought the handling up to date, and an all syn-

Left and above: The chopped rear and full-width bumpers gave the Spitfire a whole new look for the seventies with the introduction of the Mk IV. (Spitfire Mk IV 1972).

chromesh gearbox for the first time.

The last model in the line, introduced in late 1973, was not called the Mk V, but the Spitfire 1500. This may have been an attempt to distance the new model from the previous ones, now that the car was definitely showing its age. Lack of power had been the main complaint, and the new 1500cc engine would help somewhat, although the power, at just 71bhp, was not outstanding. The rear track

was also increased slightly, which enhanced the stability. The many American enthusiasts who championed British sportscars were annoyed by aspects of the Spitfire. Leyland tried to meet emissions regulations, but in a rather half-hearted fashion that gave US customers the feeling that they were poor relations. The power output from US-legal engine configurations was thought derisory - almost 30% down on the UK setup in the case of the 1500. All this af-

fected US sales - there was just so much compromise that a customer could stand. However, the Spitfire managed decent sales overall - 314,000 were manufactured in total. It is remembered as a classic, maybe not the most sophisticated car ever built, but with the one great quality that so many cars lack - it was fun!

Ken and Diana Mulhall bought their Mk III Spitfire in 1986. It was poorly finished in red, enhanced by the colour of rust, and had a distinct

The Spitfire was designed to be fun - 314,000 buyers said 'yes please.' (Spitfire Mk IV 1972).

aroma, due to the fungus mushrooming in the damp footwells and seats. A delight for all the senses! A good dry-out and clean revealed a car that needed major work, but it ran, and was used occasionally for two years before failing its MoT road worthiness test (in style). The car was stripped and the search for real metal began. There was not a great deal to be found. The Mulhalls spent many weekends at autojumbles sourcing genuine parts and panels before embarking on the reconstruction of the bodywork. The chassis was found to be basically sound, and was thoroughly treated to protect it. The finished car was professionally painted in its original Triumph white, and the interior was refurbished. The finished car, which passed its MOT first time in 1992., has since travelled to many events and collected many awards.

The boot lid of the Mulhall's Spitfire is fitted with a rack to take Ken's wheelchair. Ken is partially paralysed by Multiple Sclerosis, but is keen to encourage anyone with similar problems who might be contemplating a restoration to go for it. 'Don't despair!' says Ken. 'With a supportive wife, a little help from friends, and a number of stools of varying heights, we have now completed restoration of three cars.'

THE GT6

Around the time that Triumph introduced the Herald, in 1959, the company began to look at other projects and concepts to extend the product range and increase sales. Triumph came up with the Herald-based Spitfire, and a new engine - a six cylinder based on the Herald unit. This six cylinder engine, in 1600cc form, was fitted into a Herald that had gone back to the Michelotti drawing board for new front end treatment and a sturdier chassis. The new car, named the Vitesse, was launched in 1962 in saloon and convertible versions. With the launch of the GT6 in 1966, the Vitesse got a welcome power boost in the shape of the former's 95bhp two litre (1998cc) engine. In 1968, as

The Triumph Vitesse was a roomy little car, comfortable and fun, but it faced stiff competition in the market. (Vitesse Mk II 1971).

the Vitesse Mk II, the car got improved suspension, plus another slight increase in power from a redesigned camshaft - attributes it shared with the Mk II GT6. Although the Vitesse was a popular choice in the late sixties, it was up against stiff competition in the marketplace, and was withdrawn at the same time as the Herald, in May 1971.

1962 saw Triumph with both the four cylinder Spitfire and the six cylinder Vitesse on the books. It was reasonable to assume that the next stage might be a six cylinder Spitfire. Michelotti managed to get a quart into a pint pot with the help of a redesigned bonnet and complex under-bonnet plumbing. The GT6, fitted with the 1998cc engine giving a respectable 95bhp, was introduced in 1966. It was a sporty and practical little car, with space for luggage (though little for anyone of above average height). It was not long, however, before the GT6 got itself an entirely de-served reputation for handling badly, and anyone not used to its alarming traits could easily find themselves ditch-bound.

The Mk II GT6 (called GT6+ in the US) was introduced in 1968. The new model shared the upgrades of the Mk II Vitesse, giving it an increase in power to 104bhp, but the

Based on the Herald, the Vitesse was fitted with a six cylinder version of the Herald's four cylinder engine, and the styling was revised. (Vitesse Mk II 1971).

Although produced and improved over seven years, the GT6 never quite made good in the essential US market. (GT6 Mk I 1966).

The GT6 was, in many respects, a six cylinder Spitfire with weather protection. (GT6 Mk I 1966).

most important improvement was the overhaul of the rear suspension design (the advanced lower-wishbone set up improving the handling enormously). The Mk III came along in 1970, with an altered roofline and a much improved interior specification (as well as the same chopped tail restyling and detail changes as the Spitfire Mk IV).

The end of the GT6 told the same story as the other Triumphs of the time. Although they were popular, they failed to find a big US market, and sales just ran out of steam. The last GT6 rolled off the production line at the end of 1973.

Primula de Havilland owns a red GT6 Mk 1 that goes by the name of Lady Rouge (Primula's day-to-day transport - a modern four-door saloon - answers to the name of Monsieur Blanc - yes, it's a white car). Primula came by Lady Rouge in an unusual way. She had been driving around in an old Ford Capri for a while, and, although she loved the shape, she did not like the rust. A friend said, 'I know a car you'd love - the shape's similar, but it's got loads more character.' Primula went to see the car and met the lady (who rejoiced in the name of Wilhelmina) who owned it. Although Wilhelmina was not thinking of selling the car just then, she supposed she just

Exemplary handling was not a GT6 forte - two extra cylinders appear to have tipped the delicate balance between fun and terror. (GT6 Mk I 1966).

The GT6's 1998cc engine originally gave 95bhp, but this would later be increased to 104bhp with the introduction of the Mk II. (GT6 Mk I 1966).

Opposite - The Michelotti-styled GT6 looked good - the family likeness with the Spitfire is apparent, although the bonnet needed to be a GT6-special to allow for the bigger engine. (GT6 Mk I 1966).

Above and top right - The Mk III GT6 was treated to the same chopped rear and bumper-widening treatment as the Mk IV Spitfire. (GT6 Mk III).

might - one day. Primula, however, was smitten with the GT6, and enquired, at decent intervals, as to whether Wilhelmina had thought further about selling. Eventually, the answer was 'yes,' and Primula was the owner of her GT6 at last.

Primula drove the GT6 for a while, and then stored it away when her company gave her

a car with the job. When she decided to drive it again, she discovered that much of the rubber had perished, and so she decided that the time had come to give the car a complete new lease of life. With the help of a friendly mechanic, and encouragement from the local Triumph owner's club, Lady Rouge was restored to her former glory.

There was a tense period when Primula thought she might have to sell her pride and joy - she was without a job for a while, and had bills to pay - but happily she found a new job, and the Primula/ Lady Rouge partnership was assured. Primula would never part with her now. She is more than just a car - she's an old friend!

Quart into a pint pot - the GT6's engine was encouraged to fit with the help of some complex plumbing. (GT6 Mk III).

The elegant curves of the GT6. (GT6 Mk III).

THE STAG

The Stag was conceived as the car that would take on the competition for the Triumph name and sweep all before it. Under different circumstances, and at a different time, it might have achieved just that. Sadly, however, although the concept was good, the design elegant, and the marketing possibilities favourable, the Stag suffered from the Leyland curse of bad planning, quality problems, and a poor understanding of the US market.

The Stag was designed as a Grand Tourer, its marketing suggesting that a quick visit to one's place in the South of France would be its ideal journey. Michelotti developed the Stag around the Triumph 2000 saloon car, and it was estimated that it could easily be sold in quantities of 1000, or so, per month. Initially it seemed as though Triumph might be on to a winner. The Stag was launched in 1970, and an immediate waiting list built up. However, sales soon started to fall short of the target. This was not entirely the fault of the car, or the manu-

Opposite and above - The Stag bears a family resemblance to the TR6, alongside which it might have consolidated Triumph's sportscar expectations, had market forces not been against it. (Stag 1972).

facturer. The effects of the oil crisis hit at the crucial moment when Stag sales should have been consolidating. Had Leyland been in a healthier position, financially, there might have been hope. The Stag, however, had problems that could only have been solved by a redesign - an expensive redesign.

The US market should also have been a prime target for the Stag. However, the car's launch was delayed several times because US emission laws were tightened.

The original Stag, later to be known as the Mk I, was fitted with a three litre V8 engine giving a power output of 145bhp. The engine had serious overheating problems, though, and just one overheating episode was enough to write-off the cylinder heads. These problems were even worse in the US where the climate compounded the problems, and where there were very few mechanics trained to fix the cars. These problems led to the US market being abandoned in 1973, the same year that the Mk II Stag was introduced. The Mk II differed from its predecessor in having a slightly higher compression ratio. There were cosmetic changes too - coachstripes along the sides and black painted sills which later changed to bright metal. The Stag lasted until 1977, by which time just 26,000 had rolled off the production line - barely a third of the hoped-for total.

Although originally a Mk I, John Mumford's bright green Stag has many Mk II attributes, including its colour. Java Green was only available on the Mk II as production drew

Above and opposite: As a luxury tourer-cum-sportscar, the Stag should have been a winner, but fell foul of tightening US emission laws and an oil crisis. (Stag 1972).

to a close (in fact only around 125 cars left the factory in this colour, and John's car wasn't one of them). John's Stag, which was originally white, was supplied by Triumph dealers Clark and Lambert to it's first owner, who lived in Eastbourne, in 1972. The car was later sold to a motor trader who allegedly bought it for his wife's personal use. John bought the car - by now bright green - in 1982. At that time, John admits, he was still very naive about cars, and of course his perception was clouded by having fallen in love with this particular car. So when he asked why there was

The Mk II Stag was introduced in 1973, with cosmetic changes, such as coachstripes and black sills, in addition to minor engine changes. Like many Mk I Stags, this car carries some Mk II updating, including the stripes, steering wheel and exclusively Mk II Java Green colour. (Stag 1972).

white paint in the engine compartment instead of Java Green, he was more than happy with the response that all Stags rolled off the production line in white, and it was down to the owner to organise other colours!

John loved the colour, and the car, but felt he needed to know more about Stags. He soon joined the Stag Owners Club, where his education began - not least on the subject of original Stag paint colours! John replaced the Stag's engine, and would have liked to go for a respray too, but finances dictated otherwise. Then in 1988, John won £500 in a spot the ball competition - enough for a decent respray (complete with Mk II double pin-stripe), a new set of carpets, the smaller Mk II steering wheel and US spec headrests at the front. The car's total mileage over 26 years has been 65,000 - a figure which John adds to whenever the weekend weather is favourable.

Although there would be a Triumph-badged saloon built in the early eighties, the Acclaim, the demise of the Stag was the end for Triumph as a sportscar manufacturer. In the quarter of a century since the announcement of the TR2, Triumph made its name as a manufacturer of particularly British-style sportscars, cars which live on through the many enthusiasts and clubs which support, restore, and enjoy them.

Sales of the Stag were expected to reach 1000 per month. (Stag 1972).

(TR2 1955).

(Vitesse 1971).

(Spitfire Mk IV 1972).

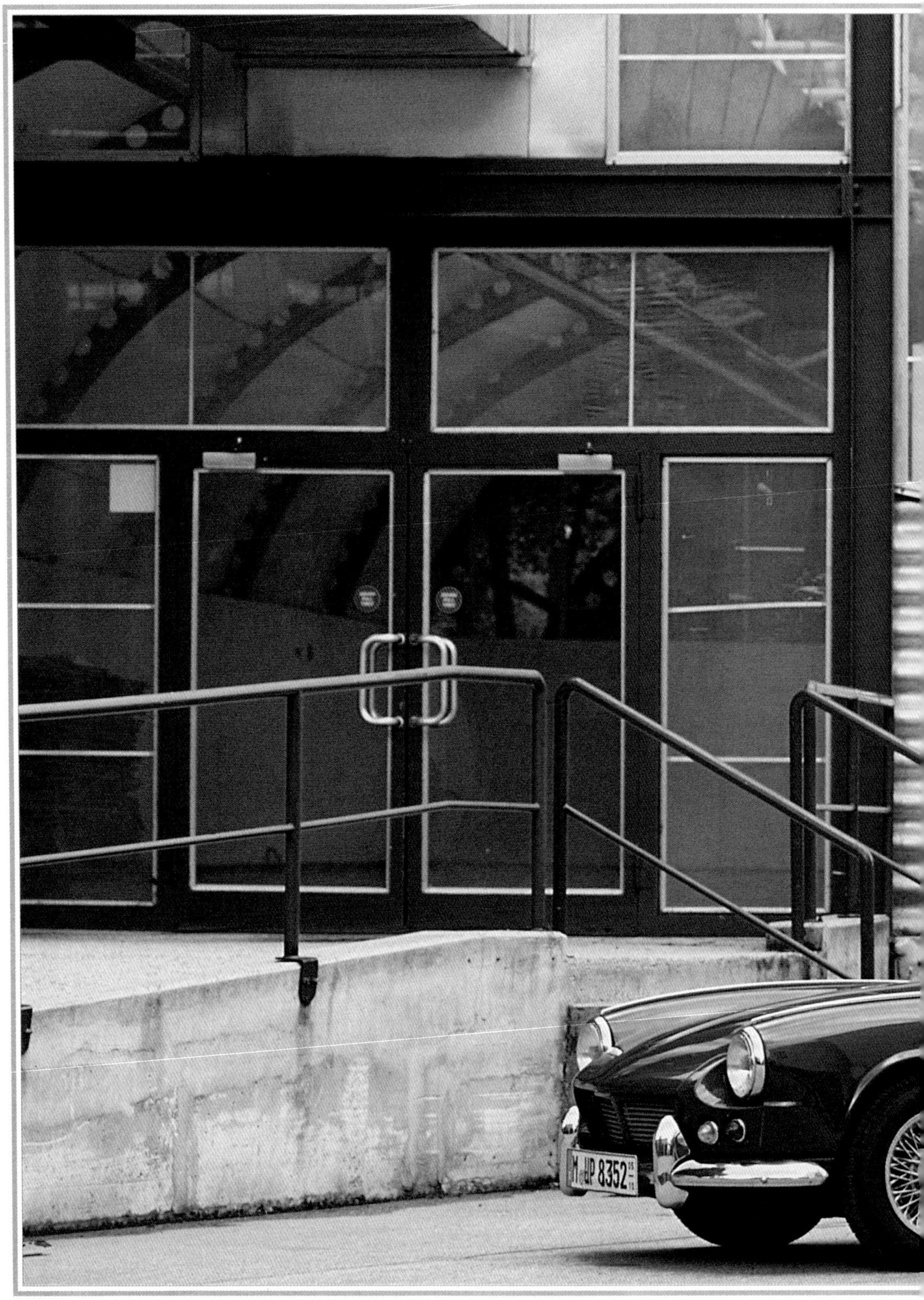

(Spitfire Mk II 1965).

(TR5 PI 1968).

PHOTOGRAPHER'S POSTSCRIPT

The idea for a book on Triumph sportscars is one that came up early during discussions on subjects for the Family Album series. I had worked on the Haynes Autofolio TR book, with Michael Roberts, during which I met Dave and Marie Lewis, and indeed photographed Dave's TR6. So when the ideas for *Family Album* subjects were being discussed, Triumph was a natural choice. I was soon on the phone to Dave, and we agreed that I would contact him when I was ready for a photoshoot. Neither of us realised at the time that we were in for a five year wait, as other subjects, anniversaries and events conspired against the Triumph book. When the day finally arrived, Dave met it in that no non-sense, no problem way that has endeared him to TR enthusiasts the world over. Almost every owner whose car is featured in this book was recommended or contacted by Dave Lewis, and it is no exaggeration to say that this book would not be what it is without his help. I must also thank Marie for the hospitality and good humour she showed me at times that were particularly difficult for her, even when the weather was cold and extremely wet.

The quality of the cars portrayed in this volume is due to the loving care and enthusiasm lavished on them by their eccentric, and often completely deranged, owners. I have never enjoyed the company of car

enthusiasts as much as I did when working on this book. Nothing was too much trouble, and it would be invidious to single out any one person.

My deepest gratitude goes to Alfred Widner, John & Mary Langford, Steve & Carol Fitton, John Sullivan, John Garlick, John Roberts, Paul Adkin, Diana & Ken Mulhall, Don & Audrey McCoy, John Canning, Dave Chambers, Eric Hines, John Mumford, Chris Balster, Lesley Phillips, Ken and Sue House, Doug and Joan Sewell, Don Pearce, Oscar Yeo, Pat Lokatis, Ralph Jones, Charlotte Weetman and Primula de Havilland. Charlotte and Primula also featured as models!

Backgrounds remain the single most problematic area for car photography, and I have been particularly fortunate with this book. I must thank the good people of Coombe Abbey for their excellent co-operation, likewise the Arrow Mill and Restaurant near Alcester, and Paul and Ann Corbett for the use of their delightful house and grounds to photograph Paul Adkin's equally delightful TR8. Ralph Jones and Charlotte Weetman's Spitfire was

photographed outside the *Slough Observer* courtesy of Peter Lawrence, the Managing Director.

In Belgium, John and Chris Vervecken-Selderslaghs' three beautiful cars provided me with an opportunity to visit Brussels airport, and some very interesting locations nearby. I am quite well acquainted with Belgian beer, but John and Chris gave me some I hadn't come across before. Magnificent!

Klaus Kistler drove me around Munich in his Spitfire, where we finally settled on the old *Messe* buildings, which sadly were about to be demolished! Thanks to you all.

Keen-eyed readers will have noticed the odd lady here and there in the pictures. Although some were owners, others were just dragged in, willingly or unwillingly (Tara Scott was a guest at a wedding, but just happened to have the ideal hat for Doug Sewell's car, Trish Black was attending a sales meeting at the time I was photo-graphing Eric Hines' magnificent TR2).

Finally, I must also thank the lovely Claudia Die de Austin, Margarita Kazala, Patricia Monson, Marie Fyfe, and last, but by no means least, Suzan Kaylan.

Film used throughout this book was Fujichrome Velvia, and the cameras were Leica R6s, with the very useful 28-70mm and 80-200mm zoom lenses, occasionally aug-mented by the 16mm Fisheye.

(Stag 1972)